ELEPHANTS

Written and edited by Jinny Johnson

Highlights

Published by *Highlights for Children, Inc.*
2300 West Fifth Avenue
P.O. Box 269
Columbus, Ohio 43216-0269

Copyright © Two-Can Publishing Ltd., 1991
All rights reserved

Designed by Millions Design
Created for Highlights for Children by
Two-Can Publishing Ltd.
London, England
Printed in the USA

ISBN 87534-217-5

Have your own monthly subscription to
HIGHLIGHTS FOR CHILDREN delivered to your
door. For information please call 800-255-9517
or write HIGHLIGHTS FOR CHILDREN, INC.,
Product Information, P.O. Box 269,
Columbus Ohio 43216-0269

10 9 8 7 6 5 4 3

Illustration credits:
p.1 Michael Woods p.6 Paul Richardson p.8 Paul Richardson
p.10-11 Michael Woods p.12-13 Paul Richardson
p.18-19 Michael Woods p.20-21 Paul Richardson
p.22 Paul Richardson p.26-30 Derick Bown (Linden Artists)

Photograph credits:
All photographs provided by Bruce Coleman Ltd.
p.4-5 Jen and Des Bartlett p.7 G. D. Plage p.9 Dieter and Mary Plage
p.13 Peter Davey p.14-15 Peter Davey p.15 Des Bartlett
p.16 Stephen J. Krasemann p.17 Jen and Des Bartlett
p.18 Jen and Des Bartlett p.20 Dieter and Mary Plage
p.23 Michael Freeman p.24 Norman Myers p.25 Gerald Cubitt

Front cover: Ardea London Ltd. (Clem Haagner)

Contents

Looking at elephants	4
Elephants in Africa	6
Elephants in Asia	8
Tusks and trunks	10
Food and feeding	12
Elephant families	14
Baby elephants	16
Growing up	18
Bathtime	20
Working elephants	22
Elephants in danger	24
Sobo's sad day	26
Elephant quiz	31
Index	32

Looking at elephants

Elephants are the biggest of all land animals and truly magnificent creatures. A male grows to eleven feet or more, about twice the height of an adult human.

Elephants live in two parts of the world, Africa and Asia. They are intelligent and very strong. An elephant has a huge, heavy body, supported on thick legs like pillars. Each of its large feet has a cushionlike pad underneath, which helps absorb the elephant's huge weight.

Elephants usually move slowly – about the same speed as a human. But they can trot very fast and overtake a human over a short distance.

An elephant is covered with thick wrinkled skin, which looks too big for its body. Some coarse hair is scattered over the body.

Elephants are very friendly and affectionate to each other. Usually elephants are very gentle creatures. But if an elephant is angry or frightened it may stampede, crashing through anything in its path like a bulldozer.

Elephants live a long time, up to fifty or sixty years in the wild. They keep growing, so the biggest elephant in a herd is usually the oldest.

▶ A family of majestic African elephants make their regular visit to a waterhole to quench their thirst and bathe.

Elephants in Africa

There are two types of elephants in Africa. One is called the savanna elephant and lives in open grassland. The other is the forest elephant, which lives in the forests of central and western Africa.

The African elephant is larger than the Indian and has bigger ears and much longer tusks. Its forehead is flat and its back dips slightly in the middle. The trunk has clear ridges or rings around it and two lips at the end.

A baby African elephant has small tusks, but its adult tusks first appear when it is about two years old. They continue to grow as long as the elephant lives. Males have larger, heavier tusks than females.

The African elephant fans itself with its huge saillike ears to keep cool. People who work with elephants can tell them apart by their ears. There are always little tears, nicks, and holes around the edges, and the pattern of the veins in the ears can be clearly seen. No two elephants have ears with quite the same vein pattern or shape.

▶ A male African elephant weighs up to thirteen thousand pounds — more than 90 people.

▼ The tusks of a male African elephant may be more than ten feet long and weigh more than an adult human.

Elephants in Asia

Indian elephants live in forests in India and parts of Southeast Asia such as Malaysia and Indonesia. They are at home both in hot tropical jungle and cool mountain forests.

An Indian elephant is usually about one and a half feet shorter and two thousand pounds lighter than its African relative and has much smaller ears. The forehead is lumpy and the back smooth and rounded. The trunk is wrinkled, not ringed, and has one fleshy lip at its tip.

Males have shorter tusks than African elephants and some have no visible tusks at all. These tuskless Indian elephants usually have particularly long and well-developed trunks instead.

Many Indian elephants are kept in captivity and work for humans. People ride on their backs and they drag and lift heavy loads. They are very good at learning and remembering commands. A working elephant in India learns more than twenty different commands, such as stop, go forward, and lift.

It is easy to see why most of the elephants in circuses and zoos are Indian elephants.

▶ Most female Indian elephants have extremely small tusks. Some have none at all.

▼ A male Indian elephant with well-grown tusks.

Tusks and trunks

An elephant's tusks are actually very large teeth. They are made of a hard substance called ivory. Elephants use their tusks when feeding, for digging up roots or taking bark off trees. They may also use them as weapons.

The long trunk is made up of the elephant's nose and upper lip. An elephant can use its trunk to smell things, just as humans use their noses, but the nostrils are right at the tip.

Trunks have many other uses. The elephant can pick leaves from the trees or plants from the ground and place them in its mouth with its trunk. An elephant could not bend its mouth to the ground because its neck is much too short.

The elephant drinks by sucking water into its trunk and then squirting it into its mouth. It may also squirt the water over its body to cool itself.

The trunk is extremely strong and can uproot a tree and carry heavy loads. But it is also very sensitive to smell and touch. A mother uses her trunk to stroke her baby.

An elephant's trunk is a nose, a gentle hand, and a strong arm. It can be used as a snorkel, too. If an elephant has to cross deep water it keeps its trunk above the surface so it can breathe even if its whole body is under the water.

▼ An elephant's tusks are very strong and sharp. This elephant is using its tusks to strip bark from tree trunks to eat.

THE ELEPHANT'S "FINGERS"
● An elephant can pick up even a tiny flower with the fingerlike lips at the end of its trunk. The African elephant has two lips at the tip of its trunk. The Indian elephant has only one.

Food and feeding

Elephants spend most of their day feeding. They need a great deal of food because they are such large animals.

Every day an elephant eats about 330 pounds of food, mostly leaves and grass. Imagine a pile of a thousand apples or 350 heads of lettuce and you will have an idea of how much an elephant eats!

In the dry season when it is hard for the elephants to find enough leaves and fresh grass, they eat twigs and branches. They tear bark from trees with their sharp tusks and dig up roots. In this way they can cause a lot of damage to plants.

Indian elephants also feed on bamboo. This is a special type of grass that grows very, very tall and has extremely thick stems.

Elephants cannot last long without water and need to drink between nineteen and twenty-four gallons a day. In the dry season in Africa there is often a drought. This is a long period when no rain falls and water is scarce. At such times elephants try to find water by digging holes in dry riverbeds with their tusks.

THE ELEPHANT'S DIGESTION

● An elephant spends about sixteen hours a day feeding. But about half this food is very hard for the body to use and break down, and is still undigested when it leaves the body.

● Elephant dung contains many seeds. As elephants move around their home range they help spread plant life.

▲ An elephant can reach high into the trees with its trunk to grasp fresh green leaves to eat. In Africa, elephants feed on more than a hundred different kinds of plants and may travel long distances in search of favorite foods.

▶ Elephants are very fond of ripe fruit as well as green plants. They also eat cultivated plants, such as maize, sweet potatoes, and manioc, and cause much damage as they feed. Elephants have been known to steal fruit and other foods from human camp sites.

Elephant families

An elephant family contains only female animals and their young. Male elephants, called bulls, usually live alone or with other males.

The females, called cows, in a family are related and may be sisters or a mother and grown-up daughters. The family is usually led by the oldest female, who may be too old to have more babies.

An old female is very important to a family. She knows all about their home area, where to find food and water, and how to avoid danger. The others can learn from her.

The elephants in a family keep together and always help another family member who is hurt or in danger. If the leader senses danger, such as a nearby lion, tiger or hyena,

she makes a warning call to the rest of her family. They gather close together with the young in the middle of the group while the leader faces the enemy.

Elephants talk to each other in different ways. They make a growling sound as a warning or to keep in touch with others who may be feeding some distance away. A loud trumpeting sound means an elephant is afraid, excited, or about to attack. A calf makes a low growling sound to let its mother know it wants to feed.

Scientists have discovered that elephants make a low rumbling sound that cannot be heard by humans. This sound is too low for human ears to pick up, but elephants can hear it from more than four miles away.

Elephants can also "talk" with their bodies. The way an elephant holds its ears, trunk, or tail means something to another elephant. An elephant holds its ears right out to say "Go away, I can be fierce." A stroke of the trunk says "I am your friend."

▲ When elephants meet they greet one another. As well as making rumbling noises, they may put their trunks in each other's mouths, click their tusks together, and flap their ears. Family members often touch one another with their trunks and rub their bodies together.

◀ The animals in a family group stay very close and do everything together. Elephants are very friendly, sociable animals and related families usually stay near one another and may sometimes travel and feed together. Groups of a hundred or more elephants may gather in a herd for a short while but always separate back to their original families again.

Baby elephants

When a female is ready to mate she helps males find her by making special calls. If more than one male appears they may have a fierce fight. Elephants can be badly hurt in such fights and can break their tusks or even kill each other. The winner of the fight mates with the female. He then goes back to his solitary life and plays no part in the rearing of the young. The female elephant cares for her baby with the help of her family.

A mother elephant carries her baby in her body for twenty-two months, almost two years. That is longer than any other animal. When it is time for her to have her baby she finds a safe spot, and other females in her family gather round to help her.

Elephants usually only have one baby at a time. Twins are rare. When twins are born, one often dies within a few months. It is probably hard for the mother elephant to produce enough milk to feed two hungry calves.

The newborn baby weighs as much as 265 pounds. It is helpless at first, but only one hour after its birth the mother and her helpers gently lift it to its feet. The baby, called a calf, takes its first unsteady steps. It finds its mother's teats, which are between her front legs, and sucks milk from them.

The rest of the family are always very interested in a new baby. Each elephant comes and gently feels the baby all over with its trunk.

A few days later the calf can walk with the herd. It must stay very close to its mother. Hunting animals such as lions, tigers, and hyenas can easily kill a young elephant.

BABY FACTS
● A newborn elephant weighs as much as two people.

● A baby elephant sucks its mother's milk with its mouth, not its trunk.

● A baby elephant may suck its trunk for comfort just like a human baby sucks its thumb.

▶ This three-day old baby elephant is a perfect miniature version of its mother but has no tusks and more hair on its skin. It is still very unsteady on its feet and often falls over or gets stuck on rough ground. It cannot see well and finds its mother mostly by smell and touch. A baby elephant explores its surroundings with its trunk and constantly touches and smells everything it comes across.

Growing up

A young elephant calf feeds on its mother's milk for two years or more. If a mother cannot feed her baby, another cow in the family will. From about three months the calf also eats some leaves and grass.

A mother elephant looks after her baby well. She must teach it many things, such as what is good to eat, how to find water, and which animals are dangerous. One of the hardest tasks for the young elephant is learning how to use its trunk. At first it finds sucking up water very difficult.

Every calf has its own personality. Some are gentle and quiet and content to stay with mother. Others are very playful. A mother will smack her calf with her trunk if it gets too naughty.

As the calf grows older it starts to explore and move farther from its mother. But she or another member of the family is always ready to come to the rescue if needed.

A female elephant usually stays with her family for life and has her own babies. But if the family gets too big, a group of females leave to make their own family. They still stay close to their original group.

Male elephants leave their mother's family when they are between ten and thirteen years old.

ELEPHANT BABYSITTERS
● A female may mate again when her calf is over two years old and feeding less on her milk. An older calf helps its mother look after younger brothers or sisters.

▽ Jumping on one another is a favorite game of young elephants. They also enjoy running and chasing one another and having mock battles. The adults in the family often join in the fun, too.

Bathtime

Elephants love water and, if possible, bathe at least once a day. They often play as they bathe and squirt water at each other through their trunks. The water helps cool their bodies.

An elephant's skin is thick but easily becomes dry and cracked. Elephants take mud baths to help protect the skin from the heat and from biting insects. An adult elephant usually scoops up mud with its trunk and throws it over its back, sides, and head. Younger elephants often get right down and wriggle in the mud until they are completely covered.

Dust baths are another way of protecting the skin. The elephant sucks dust into its trunk then squirts it all over its body. If an elephant has an itchy insect bite it picks up a stick in its trunk and uses it to scratch the itch.

Elephants usually rest in the shade for a while in the heat of the day. They also sleep at night for a few hours. Young elephants always lie down to sleep, but adults can sleep standing up.

◀ This young Indian elephant is showering himself with water to cool his body. He has very unusual tusks, which cross at the tips. Such elephants are called cross-tuskers.

Working elephants

For thousands of years, Indian elephants have been captured and trained to work for humans. They are extremely strong and learn and remember orders well.

Elephants can carry heavy loads or drag huge logs out of the forest. They carry people and take part in grand processions and ceremonies wearing beautiful embroidered cloths on their backs. In the past they have even carried soldiers into battle.

More than two thousand years ago a general called Hannibal left North Africa to invade Italy with an army of men and elephants. He traveled through France and Spain and even managed to cross the Alps. With the help of the elephants he won the first battle against the Romans. His aim was to capture Rome but nearly all the elephants died from exhaustion and illness before he could reach the city.

Even today, elephants are needed to move logs in the forests of India and Southeast Asia. It is hard to drive trucks or tractors into these dense, remote forests.

Many working elephants and the elephants seen in zoos and circuses have been born in captivity. But some are still taken from the wild. An elephant must be at least ten years old before training starts.

▶ Each working elephant has one handler who it learns to trust. The handler is called a mahout and works with his animal. It can take up to ten years to train an elephant. First the elephant must be tamed so it will obey the mahout and allow him to ride on its back. It learns to respond to the mahout's commands and practices carrying light loads. Eventually the elephant is ready to work in the forest, pulling huge trees and logs which have been cut down.

ELEPHANTS ON PARADE

● Indian elephants are often used in important ceremonies. Before the ceremony there will be careful preparations. The elephant is bathed and sprinkled with perfume. Artists then paint colorful patterns on its head and ears. A cloak is spread over its back, and necklaces and ornaments are hung around its neck and head.

Elephants in danger

There are now thought to be only 600,000 to 700,000 elephants left in Africa. This is only half the number that existed in 1980. In India and Asia there are probably about 50,000 left.

Elephants are killed by hunters for sport, or die because the areas where they live are disturbed and destroyed. But most are killed for their ivory tusks. People pay a great deal of money for jewelry carved from ivory.

In 1989 most killing for ivory was banned, and many countries agreed not to let ivory be sold. But people still kill elephants unlawfully because they can get so much money for their tusks. As long as people go on buying ivory, elephants will be killed. Only elephants should wear ivory.

Elephants are big animals with huge appetites. They need a lot of space in which to live and find enough food. As there are more and more people in Africa and Asia it is hard for countries to give elephants enough space. The land is needed for people to live on and grow food.

Most elephants now live in reserves and national parks. But there are still problems. The elephants cannot move over such a large area as they used to, and may damage the park by eating too many of the plants and trees. They feed in the same places over and over again and the plants do not have time to recover and grow back.

If there are too many elephants in a reserve some may have to be killed so the rest have enough food.

Conservation groups are trying to raise millions of dollars to help save the elephants. This money could help African and Asian countries manage big reserves and protect the animals against ivory hunters.

▶ These scientists are attaching a radio collar to an elephant. The animal has first been drugged so they can work in safety. Such collars allow the scientists to track the elephant's movements and help them learn much valuable information about the lives of elephants.

▼ Rows of elephant skulls at a Kenyan research center are a sad reminder of the thousands of elephants killed in the last twenty years.

Sobo's sad day

A day in the life of an African elephant

Sobo, a female elephant, lives on the vast grassy plains of Africa with her family. Most of her days pass quietly – feeding, sleeping, and caring for her young calf, Tatou. But one day Sobo and her family come face to face with danger.

It was early morning and the first rays of the sun were shining on the great plain that was Sobo's home. She lived there with her family – her mother and sisters and all their young. Sobo's own first baby, Tatou, was just six months old.

The elephants were on their way to drink at a stream. Sobo's mother, the oldest of the family, led the way along

the dusty path. She knew every inch of their home area. As Sobo walked, her heavy feet hardly making a sound, she watched Tatou struggling to keep up at her side. If he slowed for a moment she gently nudged him with her trunk to hurry him along. He must not keep the family waiting.

They reached the stream. Sobo dipped her trunk into the cool water, sucked some in, and neatly squirted it into her mouth. Up until a few weeks ago Tatou had always knelt and drunk with his mouth, but now he was learning to drink through his trunk. Today he dipped his trunk in the stream like his mother and managed to squirt at least some of the water into his mouth.

When the elephants had drunk enough they moved to a large muddy area near the stream. Sobo and her sisters picked up great lumps of mud in their trunks and slapped them against their bodies. This would protect them from the hot sun and biting insects later in the day.

For Tatou and his cousins this was playtime. They waded right into the mud and joyfully rolled over and over until they were completely covered. Tatou jumped on an older calf and others joined in the fun. Soon they were one big, muddy heap.

Sobo and the other mothers had finished their bath and began to move away from the mud, signaling to the calves to follow. But Tatou was having a good time and didn't want to stop. Sobo had to give him a sharp tap with her trunk before he unwillingly pulled himself out of the mud.

It was time to start feeding on the fresh plants and grasses that grew near the water. Sobo wound her trunk around a big bunch of leaves, pulled it away from the tree, and popped it into her mouth.

Tatou still fed on his mother's milk but he liked to eat some plants as well. He tried to copy Sobo but his trunk didn't always do as it was told and he found it hard to get the leaves into his mouth. From time to time Sobo would take some chewed leaves from her own mouth and place them in his.

The elephants fed for a long time as the sun rose higher in the sky. By midday it was very hot and they were ready to rest under shady trees. Tatou

and the other calves lay down on their sides and fell fast asleep. As Tatou slept he gently sucked on his trunk. Their mothers stayed standing and dozed, fanning their huge ears back and forth to keep themselves cool. Now and then they opened their eyes to check that their calves were safe.

When Tatou woke he nuzzled under his mother's body to drink her milk. She stood patiently as he fed, occasionally flicking her tail to shoo away an irritating fly. The rest of the family were munching grass again or scratching themselves against a handy tree trunk.

Two of the older calves began chasing one another and making pretend charges through bushes. They trumpeted loudly as they played. Tatou tried to copy them, and soon the whole family had joined in the game and were making a great deal of noise.

Suddenly, loud, sharp bangs rang out. The lead elephant trumpeted in alarm and frightened calves squealed. They heard another sound. The sound of a fellow elephant in pain. Sobo ran to the patch of trees from where the sound came. She thought she recognized that call. Tatou followed. He was terrified, but even more frightened of losing his mother.

Sobo crashed through the trees into a clearing and came face to face with a terrible sight. A large bull elephant lay dead, and two humans were sawing off its long tusks. Sobo knew that elephant. It was her brother Raru who had left the family a year or so before.

Sobo stamped her heavy feet and trumpeted as loudly as she could. Waving her huge ears in anger she stormed toward the poachers. Tatou stayed hidden in the bushes, hardly able to move for fear. Would these humans hurt his mother, too?

But the poachers were running for their lives. One look at the angry elephant and they forgot the ivory tusks they had wanted so much.

Sobo went over to Raru's body lying on the ground. She sniffed it and then gently stroked the dead elephant with her trunk. Tatou and the rest of the family joined her. They stood silently looking down at Raru then began to cover his huge body with branches and leaves.

At last the old female, Sobo's mother, gave the signal that it was time to move. She made a low rumbling sound, flapped her huge ears, and walked quietly away from the body.

Later that night when darkness had covered the plain and some of the elephants were already snoring, Sobo stood caressing Tatou with her trunk. How would she keep him from such dangers? She could only teach him all she knew and help him become as wise as possible. And perhaps one day humans would leave elephants alone.

Elephant Quiz

If you have read this book carefully, you will be able to pick the right answers to all of these questions.

1 Which is bigger?
  (a) African elephant
  (b) Indian elephant

2 What do elephants eat?
  (a) other animals
  (b) grass and leaves
  (c) insects

3 How much time each day does an elephant spend feeding?
  (a) two hours
  (b) six hours
  (c) sixteen hours

4 Which has bigger ears?
  (a) African elephant
  (b) Indian elephant

5 What animals does an elephant family contain?
  (a) females and young
  (b) males, females, and young
  (c) males and young

6 How does a baby elephant feed on its mother's milk?
  (a) with its mouth
  (b) with its trunk

7 Which elephants work for humans?
  (a) Indian elephants
  (b) African elephants

8 How many elephants are thought to be left in Africa?
  (a) 250,000 to 350,000
  (b) 50,000
  (c) 600,000 to 700,000

9 Where are an elephant's nostrils?
  (a) at the tip of its trunk
  (b) next to its mouth

10 Where do elephants live?
  (a) South America
  (b) Africa and Asia
  (c) Australia

ANSWERS: 1(a) 2(b) 3(c) 4(a) 5(a) 6(a) 7(a) 8(c) 9(a) 10(b)

Index

Africa   4, 6, 24
African elephant   6, 24
age   4
Asia   4, 8, 24

baby elephants   6, 10, 16
bamboo   12
bark   10, 12
bathing   20
bull   14

calf   15, 16, 18, 19
ceremonies   22
communication   15
conservation groups   24
cow   14
cross-tusker   20

digestion   13
drinking   10, 12, 18
dung   13
dust baths   20

ears   6, 8
enemies   14, 16

families   4, 14, 15, 18
feet   4
female   6, 8, 14, 16, 18, 19
fights   16
food   10, 12, 13, 18
forest elephant   6

greeting   15
growling   15

Hannibal   22
herd   15, 16

Indian elephant   6, 8, 12, 20, 22, 24
ivory   10, 24

jungle   8

lip   6, 8, 10

mahout   22
males   6, 8, 14, 16, 19
mating   16, 19
milk   16, 18, 19
movement   4
mud baths   20

nostrils   10

play   18, 19

radio collar   24
reserves   24

savanna elephant   6
size   4, 6, 8
skin   4, 20
sleep   20

teats   16
training   22
trumpeting   15

trunk   6, 8, 10, 11, 13, 16, 18, 20
tusks   6, 8, 10, 24
twins   16

weight   6, 8
working elephants   8, 22

32